I0755943

FINISHING LINE PRESS
www.finishinglinepress.com

What The World Offers

poems by

Daniel A. Rabuzzi

Finishing Line Press
Georgetown, Kentucky

What The World Offers

Copyright © 2026 by Daniel A. Rabuzzi
ISBN 979-8-89990-413-4 First Edition
All rights reserved under International and Pan-American Copyright Conventions. No part of this book may be reproduced in any manner whatsoever without written permission from the publisher, except in the case of brief quotations embodied in critical articles and reviews.

ACKNOWLEDGMENTS

Acknowledgments of prior publication:

"pinning a relic or a flower just picked" published in *SORTES*
"What The Hare Said at the Crossroads" published in *Carmina Magazine*
"Elegy for a Kingfisher" published in *Expanded Field*
"Ospreys In Casco Bay" published in *Willawaw Journal*
"Three Sightings" in *Willows Wept Review*
"Backsight" in *Sybil's Garage*

Publisher: Leah Huete de Maines
Editor: Christen Kincaid
Cover Art: Deborah A. Mills
Author Photo: Deborah A. Mills
Cover Design: Elizabeth Maines McCleavy

Order online: www.finishinglinepress.com
also available on amazon.com

Author inquiries and mail orders:
Finishing Line Press
PO Box 1626
Georgetown, Kentucky 40324
USA

Contents

The Half-light 1

What the World Offers 2

Planetary Adjustment 3

Roses are red 4

pinning a relic or a flower just picked 5

What The Hare Said at the Crossroads 6

Heron on a Houseboat 8

Elegy for a Kingfisher 9

Hello World (Cybernetic Gospel) 10

Little Thugs 11

Quow the Night-Heron 12

Ospreys In Casco Bay 13

Three Sightings 14

Pigeon Talk 15

The Wreck of the Half-Star Credulous 16

Brimborions, or, Why Poetry Arises from the Failures of History 17

Iphigenia Before Me 18

Under The Bridge 19

I too clomb an expanse so wide 20

Holding together 21

Dead Reckoning 22

Backsight 23

The Half-light

Inspired by W.B. Yeats, "He Wishes for the Cloths of Heaven" (1899)

Electric light, still a miracle,
jumps
into relief against the blue so deep we cannot name it properly.

Quavering a little, my self reflected in the windows,
a thousand squares and rectangles,
across the bridge, where the lights line up to play.

No fear of the dark, no dread for lack of sunlight,
when the buildings pull down the lambency of heaven,
arranged neatly into rows,
and rows, so many rows,
and the moon poised so prim on the spire
of the tallest skyscraper.

What The World Offers

The world says, "I have something, some *things*, for you,"
gifts you realize are gifts only after a while,
sometimes not at all
        (can you lose a gift unrecognized?)
too often late in the day
        (fluttery old owl of Minerva)
from a glance suddenly focused on the mundane,
on earthly shine, and surface-minding miracles.

Some things exist despite our prejudices:
black swans,
rings around planets,
blue eggs from hens,
the coelacanth swimming.

Even a trip to the farmer's market
can confound our expectations.

Gifts there, at just pennies a pound.

Planetary Adjustment

The kiss started out a ten, went
        straight hot west _________ flat out.

Straightened the ley lines, {big}
Settled two seasons, {time}
Centered the tropics. {movie}

We should do this again,
more often and
soon.

Roses are red

Roses are red
like ticks,
calm and unrelenting.

Roots throttle roots,
no little wort or daisy
allowed under the jacket
of thorns,
king's teeth and
queen's daggers,
haughty hitch up
to slice a finger.

pinning a relic or a flower just picked

[thoughts while viewing works by Taeuber-Arp, Schwitters, Rauschenberg, and Snyder]

if the world
    would hold

    still

for one partial
moment,

I could quick pin a relic or a flower just picked
on its membrane,
light-dancing arc retreating before me,
always just out of   reach,
also behind me,
wave above as passed by below,
ignores placidly my mightiest whisk,
my bespoke and fully wrought token,
fingerholds, handstrokes, all the elbow-grease of
once-being, twice newly been gone

What The Hare Said at the Crossroads

In the half-salt haze-lands,
Along the tween-light marches,
I met a great crowned hare at crossroads.

His flanks pale upon
An impious greywacke throne
Tall, lean and haughty,
He lowered
With his necklace golden
And eyes that saw my core.

"Which way? You ask"
He said and laughed.
"Classic choice, you know your tales,
Leftwise: briars, thorns, a 'starved ignoble nature'
Rightwise: myrtle, blooms, a salved uncommon station."

I glanced each way

[!]
[!]

My heart on fire,
Sick for his advice, yet
Shy of sly and tricksy counsel.

I glanced, I peered

[!]
[!]

My breathing raw,
My thinking wary.

"Quick now, mortal!"
He thumped one mighty foot.
"Hopscotch and widdershins!
"Left and right may turn about,
Whose left, whose right?"

So I chose too rash, in haste;
A choice once made cannot be amended.
And now I grasp to glimpse him,
His crown, pale fur and necklace gilded,
Amongst the weeds and burdock.

Heron on a Houseboat

"When you visit the realm of the heron, you are nothing more than a trespasser by his leave."
—Gerard Everosius van der Waal, De spiegel van de natuur, en andere opmerkingen en observaties over de curiosa van de wereld (Amsterdam, 1722); my loose translation.

Taller than you remember,
He recalls a time
        Before you came.

(Scanning canals, he

        Sees
                A
                        Fish

Who *doesn't* see him.)

Stopping, you try to catch
        His eye, and
        Are dismissed,
        As if an errant schoolboy,
        A delinquent dogsbody.

He returns no kindness,
        Defies admiration,
        Denies your efforts
        To ascribe nobility to him.

He is a heron, and you are

        Not.

Elegy for a Kingfisher

Inspired by "Kingfisher freezes solid as ice skaters take to frigid Amsterdam canals," by Jane Dalton, March 3rd, 2018, The Independent (U.K.) https://www.independent.co.uk/news/world/europe/kingfisher-freezes-frozen-solid-amsterdam-canal-ice-skating-a8238141.html Please click on the link for the image of the kingfisher entombed in the ice.

Down it darts, a kingfisher, a bolt of hunger unerring, an appetite driven,
In flight.
Halted even more quickly, little blue dagger,
cerulean awl,
In the clap of a frost-giant's hands.

Forever now perfect, this vector, this angle of glide.
Immaculate image, unchanging, the essence of fierce little diver,
its fire well caught.

Happy unending, held fast in the midst of your aim.

Hello World (Cybernetic Gospel)

Angel encoded,
            emergent,
Wings hastate iridium,
Pierces the
Bright-sheen eggshell,
            Nigh metallic.

She erupts,
Wreathed in cytoplasmic
Glory;
She flexes,
            surveys,
keen
To further collective
Ovular grace,
Her light.

Little Thugs

Dreams, hah, they're little thugs

bugbears and bogles
random ruffians
from who knows where?

wrong side of every track
come to despoil you
mock your morning efforts
kick over whatever reason
            you once thought you had.

Quow the Night-Heron

Quow slipped deeper into sedges,
Locked himself deep in the marsh,
Looking for his voice,
The voice he lost on a Monday,
That went wandering on a Tuesday,
Knurring and murring in the silf-straw,
Murring and mewing by itself in the weeds,
A will-o'-the-wisp with a tongue,
Muttering on a Thursday,
Mocking its owner
On a Friday.

On a Friday,
While poor Quow hunked silently,
Voicelessly,
Cross mired in solitude
Not of his making.

Ospreys In Casco Bay

How you glared as we entered your space,
away your raised wings said, away from our nest-pilings,
or your bones we'll break as our name remembers,
fillet you like a gudgeon in our claws,
shred you like a lovely hake for our nestlings' dinner,
calling for sliced glut herring,
menhaden you wished me to be,
as you flexed your night-shelving wing-crooks,
your black eyeline arrowed at me.

Three Sightings

(i) Saw-Whet Owl. (A library lawn in the middle of a city, in fall).

Like a man (one no larger than my mittened hand!)
Caught stepping out of his bath,
It stared at me:

Who was more enthralled,
On the lamp-lit edge of night
By the pines on the lawn
Where November's last cricket sang?

(ii) Black-throated Blue Warbler. (A copse on a hillside in the country, in spring).

It thought me just another shrub,
As it chased midges around the beech trunk,
A blaze of definitive blue,
Undershot with slate,
The ink of its throat limned so precisely
That it cut the air
Behind it.

(iii) Harrier. (A country-road near a creek, in spring).

Instinct turned me around,
As the hawk ellipsed the road behind.
It floated,
Three feet over water-traced fields,
Silent,
A leisurely courier of death.

Pigeon Talk

in every dialect, inventive
straight ahead, the pout
the coo-l
the flight with clap-tips
tap tap tup
swirl like ticker tape
bounce like jitney
the roust, the puff
on the bench and
under the bench
thrusting
whirring in the tongues of
chargers
tumblers
resplendent in their duds

The Wreck of the Half-Star Credulous

Love they said was a miracle, but they didn't say what kind:
indivisible, lackadaisical, unattainable?

So we steered our craft by giddy lights,
into ports skipped quaint and queer,
    tea we sipped steeped in queenbird parlors,
    spied boat-tailed wolves on distant ridges,
    cheered jugglers and mountebanks on parade,
while hailing hard the fig-seller, the wine-merchant,
in our frond-waved evenings.

Warnings came of storms adrift but nearing:
a squirm of parrots burst down a tree trunk,
shrieking as we carved our initials;
a panther purred in very tall grass,
when we sought to picnic there.

Too late
we learned miracles are indivisible from loss, from breakage,
pheasant-tail splendor reducible, chafed brittle,
suited then for framing but not much more.

The ship we launched struck the shoals we had failed to
chart,
or mapped but did not heed,
what matters is that we foundered,
arguing still about the nature of the miracle,
while the water reached our lips.

Brimborions, or, Why Poetry Arises from the Failures of History

"The poet": Charles Oldmixon, lines 112-113 of The Caliper'd Heart (1774)

People yield,
And swiftly!,
To their own deceptions—
They yearn to be deceived.

Some ask:
Is not life the better for being
Built upon a fiction,
Succoured by a fantasy,
Guarded by a lie?

Does the tree wither for lack of truth?
Does the tree blossom for lack of truth?

As the poet says,
"Follow the sine of Love/
Be guided by its Arctuations,"
Do so:
You will
Discover the genuine deceit,
Discern the authentic mirage.

Iphigenia Before Me

"O come sweet air!
To me, and only to me, as I dance
Laden with fire and burdened with iron,
Upon the track,
Where love's cavalry gallops,
Pennons of rose and of red
Streaming behind them."

"The rhinocerate loss of my spouse
Crushes the bones of my spirit,
But leaves me unable to die,
Living out of life,
Leaching out the breath,
Down to the final, far distant lie."

"Signposts of origin unknown
Now mark the way,
The glyphs of savage divinity,
Tempting me to the pyre
Where Iphigenia is burned
Over and over, her screams
Flavoring the air like lilac and gentian,
But all I want is a horse or a mule,
Something to carry me home."

"This is a memoir of the mortal casement,
So help me, dear reader,
To find my way home,
Winding as I am along the louvered crest of a hill,
Astride a mule, our feet meeting the ground,
Inch by inch, stone by bloodied stone."

"Reader, retire not before you send me
A map or a guide, please,
And oats for my mule.
We fall now,
Lost near Mount Byblos or maybe Pompeii,
Ruins of hilltops and bloodfires blocking our way."

Under The Bridge

—The first major battle of the First Punic War was fought in 262 BCE at Agrigentum in Sicily

Misunderstood and most forgotten,
I drowse under the arches of a bridge built by Romans long ago,
Listening to the trickle of water over the stones in the stream that runs by Agrigentum to the sea.

If I listen carefully still I hear swords screeching, a lightning over my veins, and
          chariots being broken,
In a war barely remembered,
Many wars in fact subsumed and misapprehended,
While we who fought not only died but lost the name of our being,
Defeat's price so high that even our ghosts are anonymous,
Save Hannibal,
For who now knows anyone from Phoenicia, or names a culture as Punic?

I too clomb an expanse so wide

Inspired by Christina Rossetti, "The Convent Threshold" (1862)

Not her sins but others all my own.

Lead-sheeted wings, buffeting
up long causeways of air,
strike sullen fires from nyxical brick.

By one dreamer dreaming
A singular fate
A fortune so rare

By one dreamer climbing
An impossible cleaving
An unextinguishable wick

No summit in sight yet, is hope overthrown?

I tell you that I tell you not.

Holding together

Rose-colored custard
calcified bits of love
adhering to kettles of bone

My heart balanced on a needle's point,
and DNA's run all to pieces

Eyebulbs grown
by a nameless farmer
aground in fields of loss

Hair of wisdom,
my roots are showing
Doubt infuses joints
hobbled by desire

My head a law of averages
My feet exceptions to the rules
Between them,
my body plays the fool

Dead Reckoning

The dead travel with us:
In the crevices, in the furrows,
In the murmurings after light.

A comfort (*),
They give us gravity so that we don't
        accidentally fly off into heaven.
They give us direction so that we don't
        inadvertently fall down into hell's mouth.

The dead book a passage:
In the avenues, down the by-lanes,
In the scurryings beyond night.

A comfort (*).

(*) Mostly.

Backsight

If you look through a dragon's eye socket,
You see what she saw
Only backwards.

Weavers unweave tapestries.
Potters pull clay off the wheel.
Smiths' bellows suck air from the fire.

Troy leaps up from the ground,
Spits the horse out of its front gate.

We are all pure again,
Unalloyed,
Elemental,
Free from all deception.

Daniel A. Rabuzzi (www.danielarabuzzi.com) has been published in, among others, *Crab Creek Review, Ghost City Review, Asimov's, Harvard Review, New Letters, Shimmer, Goblin Fruit, and Lady Churchill's Rosebud Wristlet.* Pushcart nominee. He has published two novels: *The Choir Boats,* and *The Indigo Pheasant.* He earned degrees in the study of Scandinavian folklore and early modern German and Scandinavian history. Having lived eight years in Norway, Germany, and France, he now lives in New York City with his artistic partner & spouse, the woodcarver Deborah A. Mills (www.deborahmillswoodcarving.com).

www.ingramcontent.com/pod-product-compliance
Lightning Source LLC
LaVergne TN
LVHW090542110826
845146LV00003B/1232

* 9 7 9 8 8 9 9 9 0 4 1 3 4 *